MODEL MAKING

Colin Maxwell

Consultant: Henry Pluckrose

Photography: Chris Fairclough

FRANKLIN WATTS
New York/London/Toronto/Sydney

Copyright © 1991 Franklin Watts

Franklin Watts, Inc
387 Park Avenue South
New York, NY 10016

Library of Congress Cataloging-in-Publication Data
Maxwell, Colin.
    Model making / Colin Maxwell.
      p.   cm. — (Fresh start)
    Includes index.
    Summary: Demonstrates the techniques and materials involved in making scale models, using as an example the houses, shops, and other elements of a town street.
      ISBN 0-531-14195-0
    1. Models and modelmaking—Juvenile literature.   [1. Models and modelmaking.]   I. Title.   II. Series: Fresh start (New York, N.Y.)
    TT154.M29   1992
    720'.228—dc20   90-46113
                                                                      CIP AC

Design: K and Co

Editor: Jenny Wood

Typeset by Lineage Ltd,
Watford, England

Printed in Belgium

Contents

This book describes activities which use the following:

Acetate
Advertisements (from color magazines)
Baby's breath, dried
Balsa wood (various thicknesses)
Beads (assortment)
Brush (for glue)
Cardboard (0.5mm and 1mm thick)
Compass (with cutting attachment if possible)
Construction paper (thick)
Cutting mat (cardbord)
Dish (old, for mixing glue and paint)
Dishwashing liquid
Dowel (balsa wood)
Drawing board
Dried herbs
Drinking straws
Foamcore (¼in thick)
Glue (white)
Ink (black or brown)
Kitchen knife (old, flat)
Masking tape
Modeling clay

Newspaper (for covering your work surface)
Paintbrushes
Paints
Paper – brown craft paper
       – bond paper
       – tissue paper
       – tracing paper
Pencils
Pens
Pin (with large head)
Plaster of paris
Pliers
Polystyrene (packaging)
Ruler (metal safety)
Scissors
Scrap materials
Shrink-wrap
Sponge
Spray mount
String
T-square
Tape (double-sided)
Tea bag (used, dry)
Toothpicks
Triangle (right angle)
Wire (florist's)
X-acto® (or craft knife with pointed blade)

Model making can be very messy, so prepare well and organize your work area before you start. An old table covered in newspaper is perfect as a work surface.

If possible, try to create a different "area" for each of the three processes involved in model making: 1) drawing out; 2) cutting; 3) gluing, mixing and painting.

A drawing board is ideal for drawing out. However, if one is not available, lay a clean piece of cardboard or paper on the table as a base, and run your T-square along the table's edge. The cardboard sheet can be removed when using the table for another process, then replaced when needed.

For cutting, use a thick piece of cardboard as a "cutting mat." This will protect the surface underneath. Your cutting mat should be kept as clean as possible. A similar board can be used for the messier processes of gluing, mixing and painting.

Set your tools and materials out separately so they are easy to find. Keep a box or plastic bag for odd pieces and scraps (even small ones) which may be needed during the later stages of your model. Keep a separate bin or plastic bag for garbage.

Always clean brushes thoroughly after use, and replace the tops on pots or tubes of paint or glue.

One of the delights of model making is the large range of materials that can be used. Nearly all the materials suggested in this book can be replaced by others, while still allowing you to build the models. Developing new techniques and finding new materials is all part of the fun.

This book is a guide to some basic principles and techniques for making models. Don't stop there. Create for yourself new techniques and find different materials with which to work. Above all – have fun!

Materials

The material used for the basic structure of the models in this book is foamcore (or foamboard, as it is sometimes known). Foamcore is strong, light in weight and easy to cut. Pieces join together very well and are easy to glue. The best alternative to foamcore is strong cardboard, but if you use cardboard, you will need about twice the number of **formers** indicated (see page 9). Although foamcore is more expensive than cardboard, each of the suggested models can be made from one sheet (20in x 30in).

Design

The ideas for the designs of the models described in detail in this book (a house and a store) all came from studying pictures in books and magazines and from looking closely at a variety of buildings.

Start by making the models described here, then try designing your own. Base your model on a building near where you live. Make sketches and take photographs of the building before finalizing the design.

Scale

Once you have produced your design, use a drawing of an adult person to help you decide on the size and proportion of your model.

1 The size of an adult person who would use the buildings featured in this book.

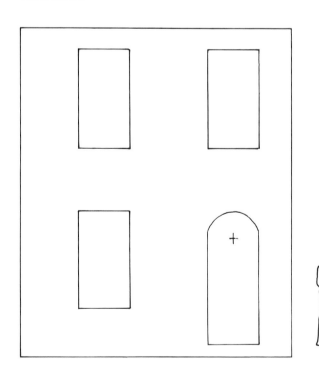

2 Use this figure to help you decide on the size and proportion of your model.

You will need a drawing board, T-square, triangle, bond paper, tracing paper, pencils, a finepoint pen, masking tape, compass (with cutting attachment if possible), a piece of foamcore 20in x 30in, a pin, a cutting mat, an X-acto® (or craft knife), a metal safety ruler, white glue, a glue brush, thin and thick cardboard, balsa wood dowel, toothpicks, paints and paintbrushes, plaster of paris, an old, flat kitchen knife, black or brown ink, a used, dry tea bag, a piece of polystyrene packaging, dried herbs, double-sided tape, tissue paper, dried baby's breath, a sponge, drinking straws, string, and balsa wood.

Drawing out

Before you start constructing the model, you must draw out the design accurately. Set up your drawing area with drawing board (if you have one), T-square and triangle. You can draw directly onto the modeling material, if you prefer, but it is usually wise to draw the design on a separate piece of bond paper or tracing paper first. Later you can add details to the design and trace details from it.

Select a piece of paper large enough for the drawing of the whole basic structure. Lightly tape it to your board or drawing base. Base your layout on the illustrations shown here. Remember that the more carefully and accurately you draw out, the easier it will be to build your model.

Use the pencil or finepoint pen to draw out the design. Always use your T-square and triangle to make sure the angles are straight. Draw the design in the following order (refer to page 9 as you work):

1 Draw the front face (front **elevation**) of the building (shown in pink on the designs), including the window and door openings. Use the compass to draw an accurate arc shape above the doorway.

2 Draw a side face (side elevation) shown in light blue.

3 Draw the other side face (yellow).

4 Draw the base (**plan**) that the house will sit on (purple). The base should be the same width as the front and the same depth as the sides.

5 Add an area for the front garden.

6 Measure the thickness of the foamcore you are going to use. This will form the thickness of the "walls." Draw in the thickness of the walls on the base (shown hatched). Draw in the thickness of the front wall on the side faces and **hatch** to remind you not to include this area when cutting out the side walls.

7 Draw in the position of the internal horizontal formers, or "floors," on the side walls, the same thickness as the walls, and draw a plan of them (light blue and light yellow stripes).

8 Finally, draw the roof. The depth should equal the length of the **pitch** at the top of the side walls. Make the width slightly larger than the width of the front elevation. Draw in the position of the side walls on the roof.

1 Here is a picture of how your finished model will look.

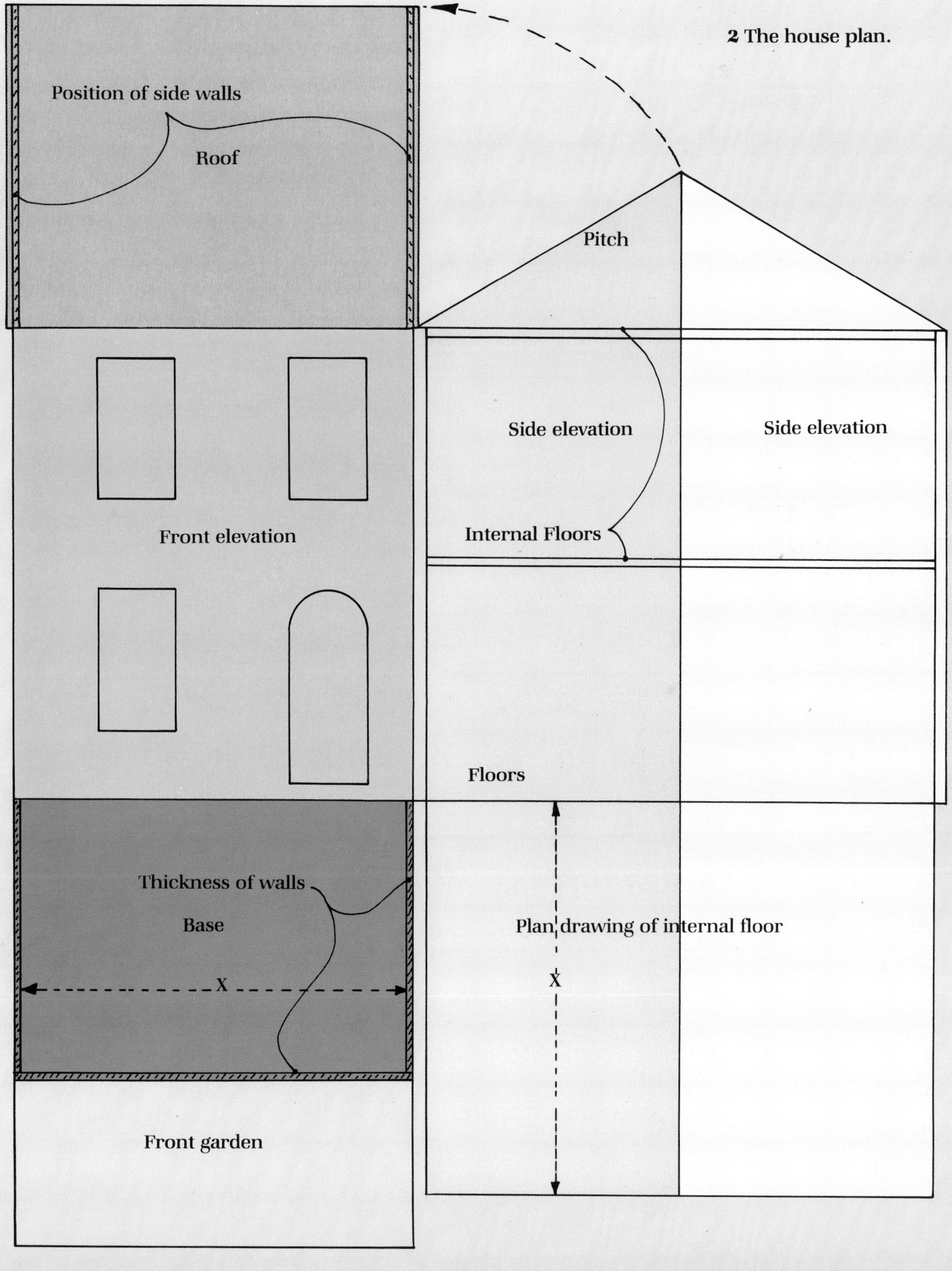

2 The house plan.

Position of side walls

Roof

Pitch

Side elevation

Side elevation

Front elevation

Internal Floors

Floors

Thickness of walls

Base

X

Plan drawing of internal floor

X

Front garden

Transferring the drawing

When you have drawn out all the pieces required to make the basic structure, transfer them on to the foamcore.

1 Place the paper over the foamcore and lightly secure with masking tape. Then take the pin and pierce through the paper at every point where lines meet.

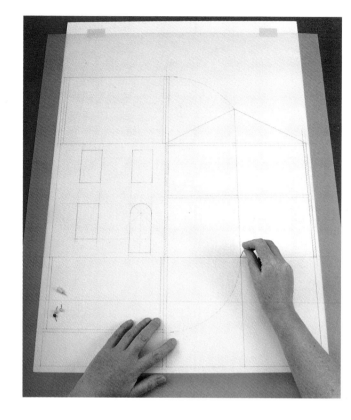

2 You will find that small pinholes appear on the foamcore.

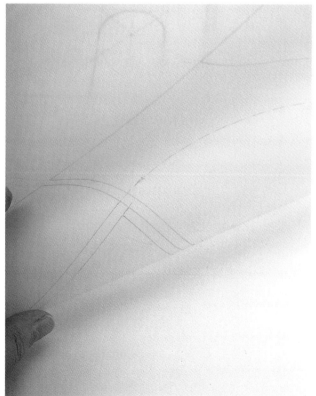

3 Join up all the pinholes to recreate the shape of your building.

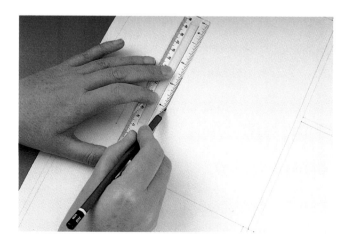

Cutting out

Now you are ready to cut. Clear away your drawing board and replace it with your cutting mat.

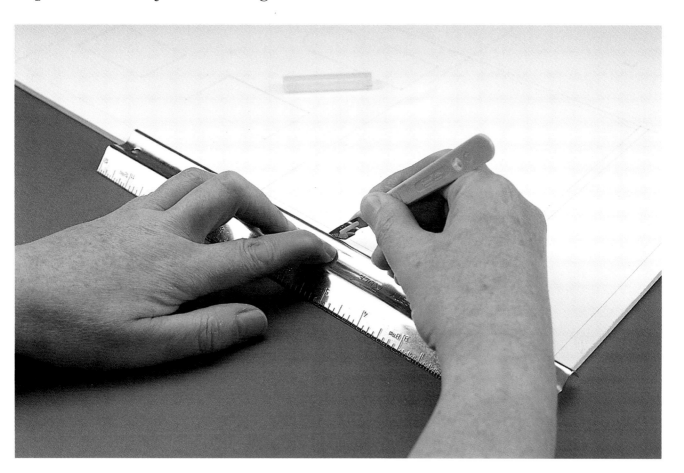

1 Place the foamcore on the cutting mat and position the metal ruler along the line you wish to cut. Position yourself directly above the ruler. Hold the X-acto® or craft knife firmly and vertically against the ruler and cut into the board. You may need to make several cuts before cutting right through the board.

BE VERY CAREFUL WHEN HANDLING OR USING AN X-ACTO OR CRAFT KNIFE.

Continue cutting until all the pieces have been cut out (do not cut out the windows or door yet). Keep the cut off pieces.

Additional marking out

Before joining the pieces together there is a little more marking out to do.

2 Use one of the side walls to transfer the position of the horizontal formers to the back of the front wall. This will help you to position correctly when gluing.

3 On the reverse side of the roof, put spacing marks (an equal distance apart) along each edge. Join with horizontal lines to give correct spacing for the roof tiles.

Take the front wall and mark out the horizontal **brick courses** along each edge (as for the roof tiles). Mark the vertical joints in the brickwork along the top and bottom edges in the same way.

Scoring

This takes a little time but, if you are patient, scoring is an excellent way of making effective "brickwork" that looks extremely realistic when painted.

Take the marked-out front wall and, instead of joining the marks with pencil as for the roof tiles, take your ruler and turn your X-acto® or craft knife over. Using the back of the blade, score lines between the marks, as though you were cutting, to form the horizontal courses.

4 Do the same with the vertical joints, skipping every other row to form a brickwork pattern. (Look closely at some real brickwork, if you are not sure about how the pattern should look.) Do the sides as well as the front of the house, if you like.

5 Now finish cutting out the window and door openings. Use a cutting attachment with your compass, if possible, to get a smooth, even cut around the door arch.

6 You may need to make some extra cuts into the corners and around the door arch before finally lifting out the pieces.

Gluing the basic structure

You are now ready to glue the pieces together. To avoid complications, try to follow the order shown here.

1 Using a small brush, spread the glue fairly generously along the bottom edge of the front wall. (Use the glue directly from a dispenser if you find it easier.)

2 Carefully place the front wall along the line drawn on the base, hold in position and press firmly. Be patient. It may take a little while for the glue to set.

3 Now position one side wall. Glue both the bottom edge and the short vertical edge, attaching these to the base and to the back of the front wall respectively. Glue the first horizontal former in place, too, and allow to set.

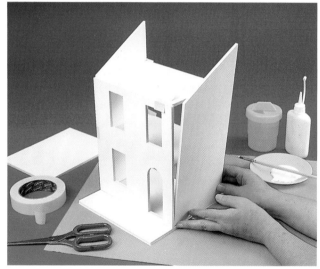

4 Position the second former, then attach the other side wall. Use masking tape, if necessary, to hold a piece in position while the glue hardens.

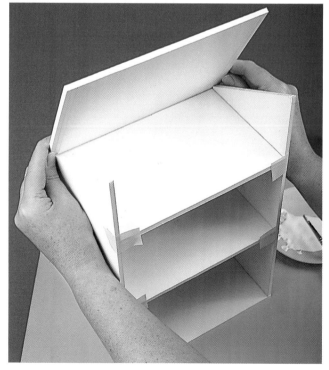

5 The roof completes the basic structure.

Painting

You should now paint the basic structure before fitting any additional features such as the windows and door.

The photographs continue to show unpainted sections, to make the instructions easier for you to follow, but you should paint the various pieces as you make them, following the directions given in the captions.

1 Use a sponge to dab paint on to the walls. Repeat, adding patches of darker and lighter shades and perhaps different colors. If you look closely at some real brickwork, you will see that there are many different shades and colors in the bricks.

Adding details to the basic structure

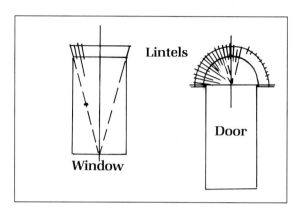

Lintels

Door

Window

1 Now return to your drawing. Overlay some tracing paper on the window and door openings and draw out the **lintels.**

2 Transfer the drawing onto thin cardboard or thick construction paper using the pin method (see page **10**). Score the brickwork (see page **13**), radiating from a single point. Cut out, paint, then glue into position.

3 Use a scrap piece of foamcore to make the windowsills. Paint the sills, gluing them into position when dry.

4 A thin strip of cardboard forms a **plinth.** Paint this, then glue it into position.

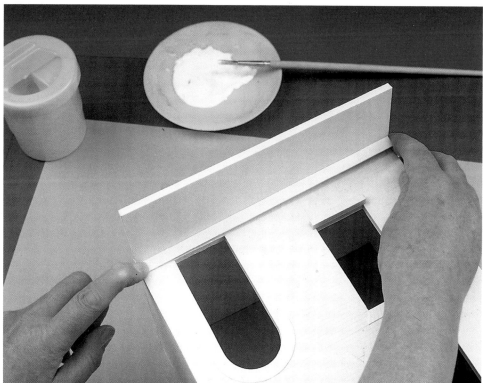

5 Draw the pieces for the chimney (front, both sides, back and top). Remember to allow for the thickness of the material.

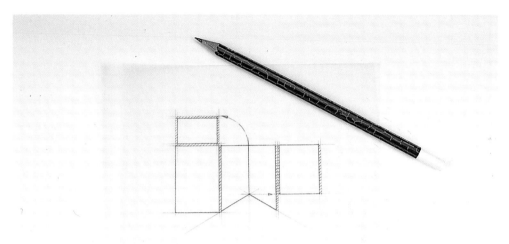

6 Transfer your drawing onto thin cardboard, and score on brickwork. Cut out the pieces and glue together. Balsa wood dowel and string make good chimney pots, and you can add some scored cardboard strips to build up a **corbel** at the top of the stack.

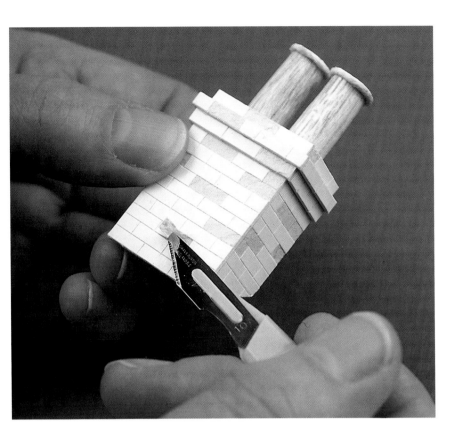

7 Removing the surface of some of the "bricks" creates a more uneven finish.

8 Paint the chimney, then fit it into position.

9 Take a piece of thin cardboard or thick construction paper and mark out a grid the size of the roof tiles. (The size of the tiles should be larger than the spacings you have already marked out on the roof. This means that they can be overlapped.) Score lines in one direction on the grid and cut strips in the other direction. These strips will form courses of tiles.

10 Starting from the bottom, glue the roof tiles into position, following the lines drawn. Overlap each course. Cut the courses around the chimney, and trim the edges.

11 Make **ridge tiles** by cutting pieces of toothpicks and gluing these onto a strip of cardboard. Brush a very watery solution of paint over all the tiles, as a base. When this is dry, brush a stronger solution of paint unevenly over the tiles, to make them look like slate.

Making the windows and door

1 Draw out one window and the door on a tracing overlay. Include the other window openings and the inside area on the tracing. Transfer the drawing to cardboard by rubbing the reverse of the drawing with a soft pencil, then, with the drawing right side up, retracing the lines using a harder pencil and ruler. There are two layers to the windows and door so you will need to transfer two images of each piece (one for each layer).

2 Cut out the first window and the door very carefully, stopping slightly short at the corners so as not to cut right through part of the frame. You may need to make several cuts to get through the cardboard. Now cut into the corners and snip out the pieces.

3 Glue the two layers together.

4 Use the door cut from the top layer as the panel backing.

5 Glue the inner door panels in position (these are cut from the second layer).

6 Check that the completed piece fits, by inserting it at the back of the structure. Repeat the same procedure for the other windows. If you wish to glaze the windows, see page **38**. Paint the door and all the windows, then glue in position.

7 The completed, unpainted structure with windows and door in position.

The front garden

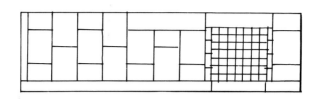

1 Begin by drawing the base plan of the garden onto an overlay.

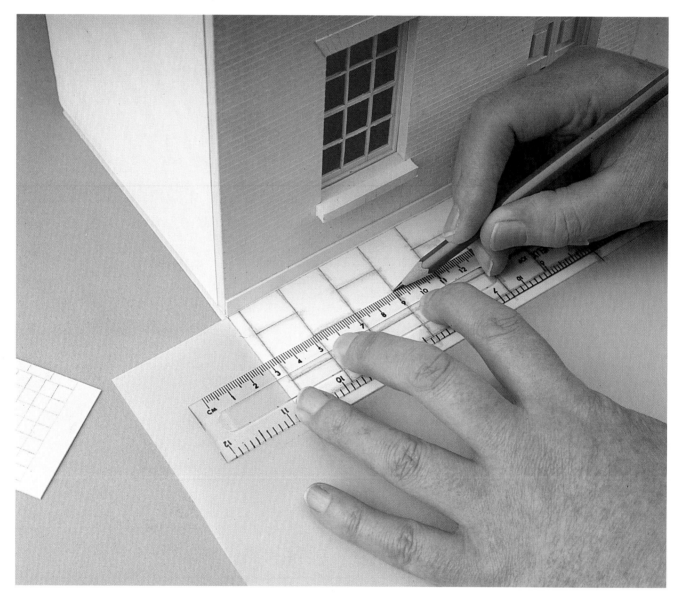

2 Transfer the tiled path drawing onto a piece of strong cardboard and cut it out. Transfer the remainder of the drawing directly onto the baseboard.

3 Mark out a grid on different colored (or painted) papers and cut out tiles to the same size as on the drawing. Glue the tiles to the path, making a pattern. Copy one of those shown here, or try making your own pattern. Glue the path to the base.

4 To introduce some texture to the model, make **flagstones** for the garden using plaster of paris. Mix the plaster according to the instructions on the package. Then, using an old kitchen knife or metal ruler (which should be wet), spread a thin layer onto two pieces of strong cardboard, each one the same size as the garden base plan. Do not worry about making the filler smooth. The rougher it is, the better the texture. Leave to dry. The cardboard may start to curl a little as it dries, but this does not matter!

5 When the cardboard pieces are dry (approximately 4 hours), take one piece and mark out a grid (the other piece will be used later – see page **29**). Cut out the flagstones, using an old blade in your X-acto® or craft knife. Try bending some of the pieces you have cut. This breaks the filler, producing cracks in the stones. Now paint the flagstones, using a very weak solution of black or brown paint or ink. A light wash is all that is required – you do not need a lot of paint to create an effect, because the plaster has already provided texture. Don't forget to paint the edges.

6 Glue the flagstones onto the base.

7 Cut pieces of strong cardboard to the size of the flower beds, and paint them black. When dry, apply some white glue and sprinkle with tea from the used tea bag, which has been allowed to dry out. Allow the glue to harden, then shake off any surplus tea. Glue the flower beds into position on the base.

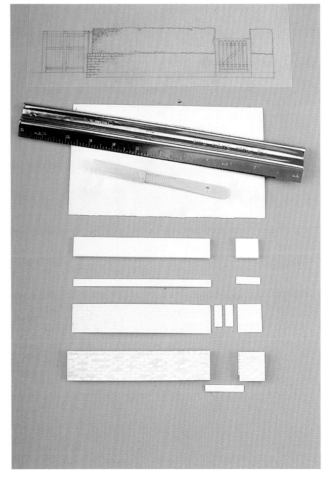

8 The garden design includes a low wall with a hedge on each side of a gate, and a fence on one side. Use the second piece of cardboard you textured with plaster to make the low wall. Score the brickwork, using an old blade (see page **13**), then glue the pieces of the wall (front, side and top) onto a foamcore backing. Paint the wall before gluing in position.

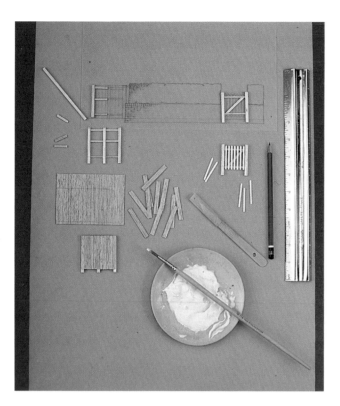

9 Cut different thicknesses of balsa wood and cardboard to make the fence and gate, using your drawing as a pattern. Paint, then glue into position.

10 For the hedge, take a piece of polystyrene packaging and cut out your shape. Use a sawing motion to achieve a clean, smooth cut. (An adult can help you do this safely.) Here, the shape has been cut to fit over the wall. You could try making different shapes, as in **topiary.** Take a pencil and puncture the piece of polystyrene heavily until the surface becomes "knobbly" all over.

11 Paint your hedge black or dark brown, making sure you get into all the crevices. When dry, cover the surface with glue. Sprinkle dried herbs (marjoram is especially good) onto the wet glue. Leave until the glue dries, and shake off the surplus. Repeat this procedure if you want to create a bushier hedge.

Making a trellis and rambling rose

Decorate your house by adding a rambling rose on a trellis around the door. Transfer your overlay drawing of the trellis onto a piece of cardboard and use the cardboard as a pattern.

Surround the drawing on the pattern with double-sided tape (or glue) and position thin strips of balsa so they are held by the tape on each side of the drawing. When you have attached one layer of strips, glue another layer on top. The strips in this second layer run in the opposite direction. Cut out the trellis and use some horizontal strips as supports to stick the trellis onto the wall.

Cut some thin strips of tissue paper (different lengths) and twist them into stems. Leave the ends untwisted for joining. Prepare a watered-down solution of glue and use this to join the stems together, twisting as you go. Paint the finished stem and glue it in position on the trellis. Dab with glue and sprinkle on herbs for leaves.

1 To make the roses, cut some heads from baby's breath, if this is easily available to you, or roll up some tissue paper and cut off small pieces.

2 The finished garden, seen from the side.

3 The finished garden, seen from the front.

4 The finished house and garden, before the two pieces are joined together. Notice some additional items: a drainpipe and fittings made from a drinking straw and string; rounded edges on the doorstep and drainpipe **gully**, to create a worn look; a few herbs sprinkled on the garden to look like weeds; and curtains made from tissue paper stiffened with glue.

5 The finished model.

Other features
Think of other things you see on a house, such as a door knocker and television antenna, and try to make these from items in your box of scrap materials.

The store (a general store) is made in almost exactly the same way as the house. You will need a drawing board, T-square, triangle, construction paper, tracing paper, a pencil or finepoint pen, masking tape, a piece of foamcore 20in x 30in, a pin, a cutting mat, an X-acto® (or craft knife), a metal safety ruler, white glue, a glue brush, thin and thick cardboard, paints and paintbrushes, **shrink-wrap** packaging or a sheet of acetate, Spray mount, florist's wire, pliers, beads, drinking straws, balsa wood, advertisements from color magazines, tissue paper, modeling clay and brown craft paper.

Follow the same procedure for making the store as you did for making the house. Draw out the design, transfer the drawing onto foamcore, cut out the pieces, score the brickwork and glue together the basic structure. Then create the features described.

To make it simpler, the photographs show unpainted sections. However, when making your own model, you should paint the pieces before gluing them together. Paint the covers before attaching the glass to them, for example, and make your window display (see page 41) before attaching the glass covers.

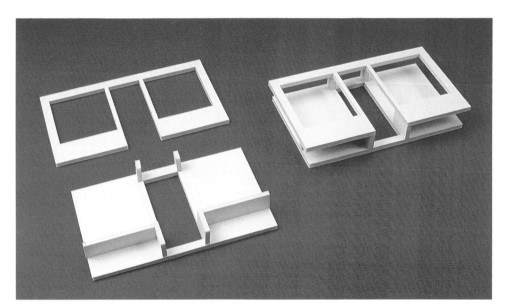

1 Here is the basic structure of the store window made from foamcore. On the left are the individual pieces, and on the right is the finished assembly.

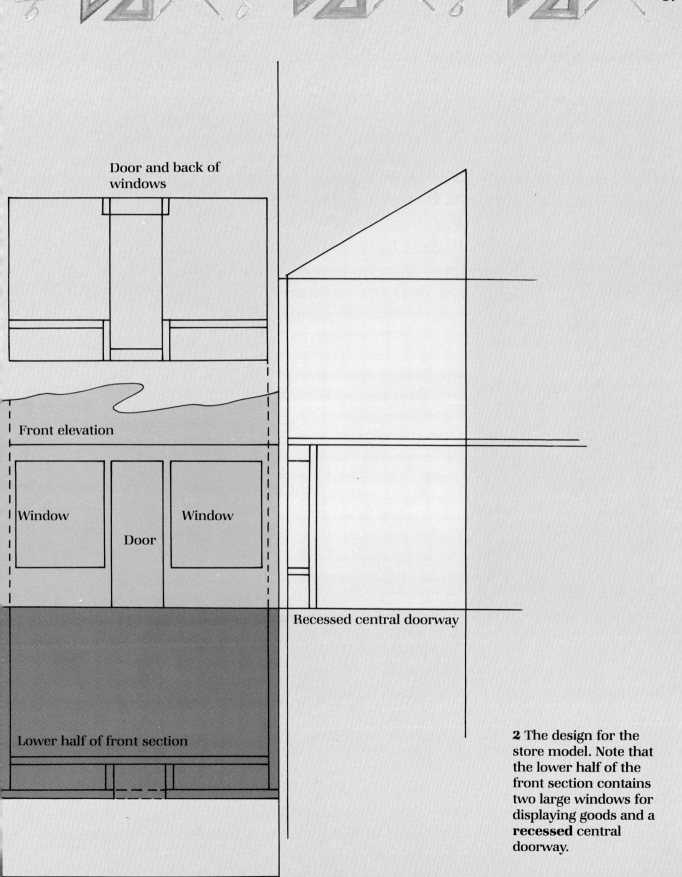

Door and back of windows

Front elevation

Window

Door

Window

Lower half of front section

Recessed central doorway

2 The design for the store model. Note that the lower half of the front section contains two large windows for displaying goods and a **recessed** central doorway.

Making the windows and door

To make windows, cut pieces of "glass" a little larger than your window openings from old pieces of shrink-wrap packaging or a sheet of acetate. Make a "cover" from cardboard the same shape as the front of the basic structure (but a little higher to allow for the **fascia**). The "glass" can be stuck to the back of this. Make small pieces of "glass" for the sides of the windows in the door recess. Do not attach these yet.

The door is made in the same way as the door in the house (see page 23), but using a "glass" panel. You can create a frosted glass effect by spraying the packaging or acetate with spray mount (if you use this, ask an adult to help you). You can also make a small shade for the back of the door.

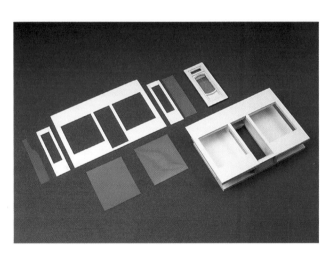

3 Here you can see the glass pieces with their covers (on the left), and in position (but not attached) on the basic window (on the right). You can also see the finished door.

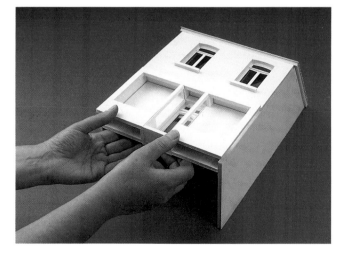

4 Fit the basic window into the main building with the door in position (but not attached). Add a foamcore step in the door recess. Note that the style of the upper windows differs from those used in the house, but you can use whichever design you prefer. Look at some buildings near where you live – you will see that windows come in all shapes and sizes!

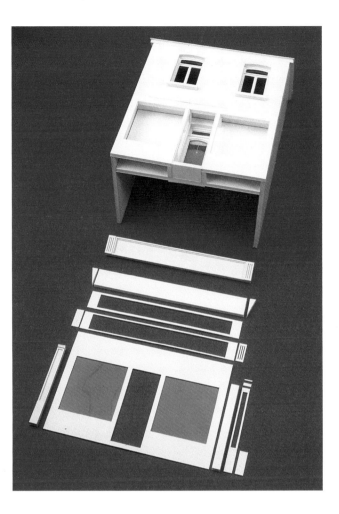

5 In the foreground of this picture is the front cover with the glass, showing side pillars and a store sign made from cardboard. (You can stick these details onto the front cover at this stage.) In the background you can see the building with the basic window fitted. (Do not stick the cover to the main structure yet, however, as you will need to do work inside the windows.)

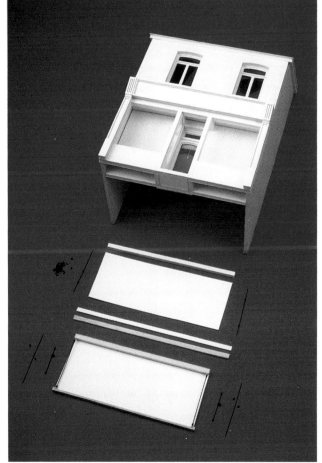

6 Here you can see the completed store window in position (but not attached) showing the makeup for the **awning.** The pieces are shown in the center of the picture, and the assembled awning is shown in the foreground. Use construction paper or fabric for the shade, and florist's wire for the metal supports (this wire can be cut easily using a pair of pliers). Small beads make very good imitation joints and fixings. Study the finished assembly on page **43.**

7 Make some packages, boxes, bottles and cans for the window display using straws and balsa wood cut into small pieces. Cover the objects with pieces of advertisements cut from old color magazines to make them look really authentic. Small trade names cut from magazines also make good signs.

8 You can also make a bulletin board using small pieces of paper for advertisements.

9 Display produce in the finished window on boxes made from foamcore covered with tissue paper that has been strengthened with diluted glue. Score tiles into the cover and use a thin strip of cardboard as a windowsill.

10 You could almost walk through the door!

11 Add extra details such as a vegetable stall outside the store. Make the stall from balsa wood, following the method used for the gate and fence outside the house (see page **30**). Make tomatoes and potatoes from small balls of modeling clay, a sack from brown craft paper, leeks from twisted pieces of tissue paper, cabbages from screwed-up pieces of tissue paper, and carrots from chips of balsa wood. Paint all these objects to complete the effect.

12 The finished stall in position outside the shop.

13 You may need a stronger glue to attach the awning.

14 Try rescoring the brickwork to accentuate the **pointing.**

15 The finished store.
You might like to give
your store a name.

An old, run-down service station makes an excellent contrast to the previous two models, although again it is made in the same way.

The basic structure is made from foamcore. Wooden beams made from strips of balsa wood have been added to the front of the roof, and a textured brickwork effect has been created on the walls (see page **13**).

Corrugated paper acts as a realistic garage roof, while strips of balsa wood glued onto cardboard make strong wooden doors. Tracing paper in the windows makes effective dirty glass, while trade names cut from magazines serve as signs (see page **40**). The gasoline pump is made from foamcore, cardboard, wire and beads.

When you are feeling confident, try making a more complicated building such as this town hall. Follow the same process as before, but add extra details and decorations. Use strips of cardboard, balsa wood, string, blocks of foamcore, and paper doilies to make these.

The balcony balusters are made by pouring dental plaster into a shaped modeling clay mold, and letting it dry. Shape the mold by pressing beads, nuts and buttons into the modeling clay.

Having attempted to make the models in this book, you will probably have learned that there are no set rules. Every model you attempt will pose a different set of problems and demand new techniques for you to invent.

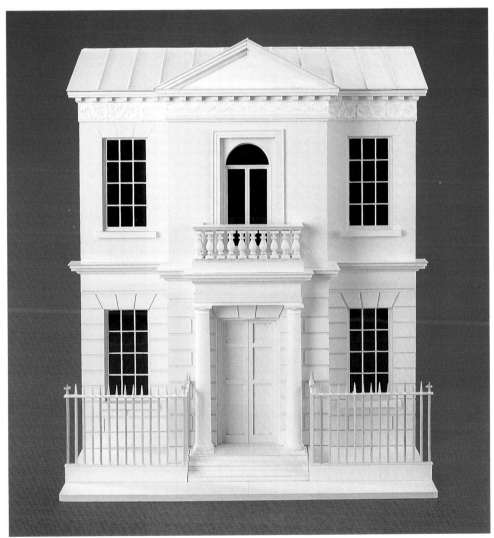

1 "Casting" is an easy way of making a number of identical objects, such as balusters. To make a "master" baluster, bend open a paper clip and stick it into a clay stand. Feed beads, nuts and buttons onto the clip to form the baluster shape. Glue in position and allow to dry. Prepare some clay "tablets." Press the "master" baluster halfway into each tablet to make an impression, then use a metal ruler to smooth and flatten the surface of each tablet. These shaped tablets will act as molds. Rinse the molds in a bowl of water to which has been added a squirt of dishwashing liquid. Prepare some dental plaster and brush this into the molds. Tap the molds gently on the table to remove air bubbles. Lay a short length of wire in each mold and leave to dry. When dry, pull away the clay and lift out the cast shapes. These are "half" balusters. Stick two halves back to back to make a whole baluster.

Most of the basic materials and tools required for making the models in this book can be obtained from any good artists' materials store.

Supermarkets stock toothpicks, drinking straws and herbs. Florists stock garden wire and baby's breath. Variety, notion and fabric stores stock buttons and beads.

Some drugstores stock dental plaster, but other casting plasters are available from most art supply stores. (NB: DO NOT USE PLASTER OF PARIS FOR FINE CASTING WORK.)

Large quantities of balsa wood can be obtained from home centers and lumberyards.

Large quantities of artists' materials can be ordered through most art supply stores.

Keep a lookout for items and materials around the home which might be useful for making models. Save polystyrene (styrofoam) and vacuum-formed packaging from store-bought goods.

Some applications of model making

Here are some examples of the ways in which models are used.

Architecture: A model is used to show what a building will look like, before construction begins.

Engineering: Working models are used to test various stresses that act on an object. A model of an airplane in a wind tunnel, for example, will help the engineer decide on the shape of the wings.

Movies and television: As a way of saving time and money, a model may be used to avoid having to construct a full-size scene. The model is then filmed so that it seems life-size. Mechanical and animated models are often used for special effects.

Museums: Models are sometimes used to depict a scene from the past. Many museums have models that move. Some show how different machines work, others demonstrate scientific principles.

Theater: Designers make models of the scenery for a production, to demonstrate the scene changes. These models look rather like toy theaters.

Architectural terms

Awning – a canopy outside a store.

a column sits.

Brick course – a horizontal row of bricks of the same height.

Corbel – a projecting course of brickwork.

Fascia – the name board above a store.

Flagstones – stones used for paving.

Gully – a drain at the bottom of a drainpipe which collects water.

Lintel – a beam placed over a doorway or window to support the wall above it.

Pitch – the slope of a roof.

Plinth – a projecting strip at the base of a wall.

Pointing – the mortar between joints in brickwork, binding the bricks together.

Recess – a part that is set back from the main face of a building.

Ridge tile – a tile on the upper angle (ridge) of a roof.

Modeling/drawing terms

Elevation (front/side) – a drawing of a vertical face looking at it at 90°

Former – a shaped piece of cardboard that forms a support for the structure of a model.

Hatch – shade with parallel lines.

Plan – a drawing of a base looking down on it at 90°.

Other terms

Shrink-wrap clear plastic film formed around an object by using a heating process.

Topiary – the art of cutting trees or shrubs into shapes.